Grasshoppers

and Their Relatives

Editor in Chief: Paul A. Kobasa
Supplementary Publications: Christine Sullivan, Scott Thomas
Research: Cheryl Graham
Graphics and Design: Sandra Dyrlund, Charlene Epple
Permissions: Janet Peterson
Prepress and Manufacturing: Carma Fazio, Anne Fritzinger, Steven Hueppchen, Tina Ramirez
Writer: Patricia Brennan
Concept and Product Development: Editorial Options, Inc.
Series Designer: Karen Donica

For information about other World Book publications, visit our Web site at
http://www.worldbook.com or call 1-800-WORLDBK (967-5325).

For information about sales to schools and libraries, call 1-800-975-3250 (United States);
1-800-837-5365 (Canada).

World Book, Inc.
233 N. Michigan Avenue
Chicago, IL 60601

The Library of Congress has catalogued an earlier edition of this title as follows:

Grasshoppers and their relatives.
     p. cm. -- (World Book's animals of the world)
   ISBN 0-7166-1219-4 -- ISBN 0-7166-1211-9 (set)
   1. Grasshoppers--Juvenile literature. 2. Insects--Juvenile literature. [1. Grasshoppers.
2.Insects.] I. World Book, Inc. II. Series.

   QL508.A2 G74 2001
   595.7'26--dc21   2001017521

This edition:
Set 2 ISBN-13: 978-0-7166-1351-0   Set 2 ISBN-10: 0-7166-1351-4
Grasshoppers ISBN-13: 978-0-7166-1345-9   Grasshoppers ISBN-10: 0-7166-1345-X

Printed in Malaysia

3 4 5 6 7 8 9 09 08 07 06

Picture Acknowledgments: Cover: © Norman O. Tomalin, Bruce Coleman Inc.; © Joe McDonald, Tom Stack & Associates;
© Laura Riley, Bruce Coleman Inc.; © David M. Schleser, Photo Researchers; © Peter Ward, Bruce Coleman Inc..

© A. Cosmos Blank, Bruce Coleman Inc. 53; © Waina Cheng Ward, Bruce Coleman Collection 27; © Ray Coleman, Photo Researchers
19, 43; © Stephen Dalton, Photo Researchers 5, 15; © Kent & Donna Dannen, Photo Researchers 9; © John Fennell, Bruce Coleman
Inc. 59; © Stephen J. Krasemann, Photo Researchers 9; © Dwight Kuhn, Bruce Coleman Inc. 55; © Daniel J. Lyons, Bruce Coleman
Inc. 25; © Joe McDonald, Tom Stack & Associates 37; © Joe McDonald, Bruce Coleman Collection 29; © Kenneth Murray, Photo
Researchers 9; © Nuridsany & Pérennou from Photo Researchers 33; © O.S.F. from Animals Animals 57; © Rod Planck, Photo
Researchers 9; © Laura Riley, Bruce Coleman Inc. 7, 61; © J. H. Robinson, Photo Researchers 3, 21; © Edward S. Ross 39, 49;
© Steve E. Ross, Photo Researchers 13; © David M. Schleser, Photo Researchers 5, 47; © Keren Su, China Span 45; © Gianni Tortoli,
Photo Researchers 23, 35; © Jerrold & Linda Waldman, Bruce Coleman Inc. 17; © Peter Ward, Bruce Coleman Inc. 4, 31; © Doug
Wechsler, Animals Animals 51; © Gary R. Zahm, Bruce Coleman Inc. 41.

Illustrations: WORLD BOOK illustration by Michael DiGiorgio 11, Karen Donica 62.

World Book's Animals of the World

Grasshoppers
and Their Relatives

World Book, Inc.
A Scott Fetzer company
Chicago

Contents

What Are Grasshoppers and Their Relatives?

There are over 1 million different kinds of insects in the world. Grasshoppers belong to a group of insects called orthoptera *(awr THAHP tuhr uh)*. Katydids *(KAY tih dihdz)* and crickets also belong to this group.

Most of these insects can do amazing leaps. The grasshopper you see here is about 1 inch (2.5 centimeters) long. But it can leap 20 inches (50.8 centimeters). If a person 5 feet (1.5 meters) tall could jump that well, he or she could leap from one end of a basketball court to the other.

Orthoptera are also known for their musical talents. Many communicate by sound. And they have unusual ways of making their "songs."

Like all insects, orthoptera have three pairs of legs. To spot an orthopteron, look at its two hind legs. They are longer than the other legs. Powerful muscles in its back legs help an orthopteron leap.

Grasshopper

Where in the World Do These Animals Live?

These animals live almost everywhere on land. They live in forests, grasslands, and deserts. They even live on mountains. But there are two places where they don't live—the freezing North and South poles.

Why not? Because orthoptera need warm bodies in order to survive. Like all insects, orthoptera are cold-blooded. That means the temperature of their bodies changes with the temperature of the air. If it's hot outside, the insect's body is hot. If it's cold outside, the insect's body is cold. If it's too cold, the insect could freeze solid.

Did you ever notice when grasshoppers jump the most? They jump most in the middle of a hot afternoon. During the cool morning, they stay still. That's because grasshoppers and other insects can't be very active until their bodies warm up.

Forest

Grassland

Desert

Mountain

How Is a Grasshopper Put Together?

A grasshopper's body has three main parts. They are the head, the thorax *(THAWR aks),* and the abdomen. A stiff shell called an exoskeleton *(EHK soh SKEHL uh tuhn)* covers the body.

A grasshopper has its eyes, mouth, and antennae *(an TEHN ee)* on its head. It may look as if this insect has just two big eyes. But it really has five eyes.

A grasshopper's two large eyes are compound eyes. They are made up of many separate lenses. The lenses work together to form a complete picture. A grasshopper uses its compound eyes to see. Scientists aren't sure how a grasshopper uses its smaller eyes.

The thorax is the middle part of a grasshopper. The legs and wings are attached here. The abdomen is the back part. A grasshopper has breathing holes on its thorax and abdomen. These holes are called spiracles *(SPY ruh kuhlz).*

Diagram of a Grasshopper

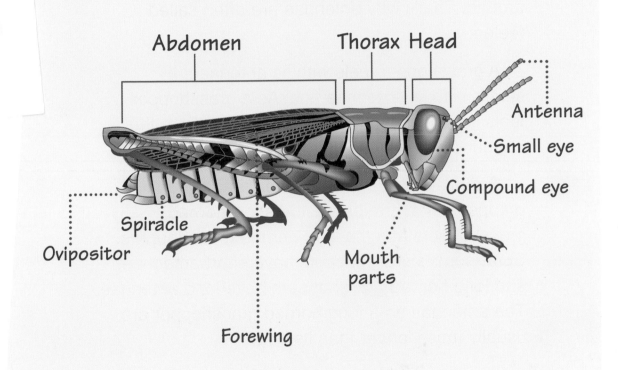

Abdomen

Thorax Head

Antenna

Small eye

Compound eye

Spiracle

Oviposator

Mouth parts

Forewing

How Do Some Grasshoppers "Feel" Around?

A grasshopper's antennae are thin and very sensitive. They help the grasshopper feel its way around. That's why antennae are often called feelers.

A grasshopper feels with its antennae. It smells with its antennae, too. As a grasshopper feels its way around, it picks up scents from the surroundings.

Scientists divide grasshoppers into two main groups. These groups are the short-horned grasshoppers and the long-horned grasshoppers. Short-horned grasshoppers have short antennae, and long-horned grasshoppers have long antennae. The antennae on a long-horned grasshopper are usually much longer than its body.

Long-horned
grasshopper

How Does a Grasshopper Move About?

A grasshopper uses its legs and wings to move about. To walk, a grasshopper uses all six of its legs. To leap, it pushes off with its long, strong back legs. The grasshopper in the photograph is shown both before and during a leap. You can see how the grasshopper's back legs propel it forward. Or, the grasshopper may shoot straight up into the air.

Many grasshoppers with wings can also fly. These grasshoppers use their back wings for flying. They use their wings in much the same way that a bird does.

Some grasshoppers have wings they can't use. A few kinds never grow wings. These grasshoppers can't fly. It's a good thing they can leap so well!

14

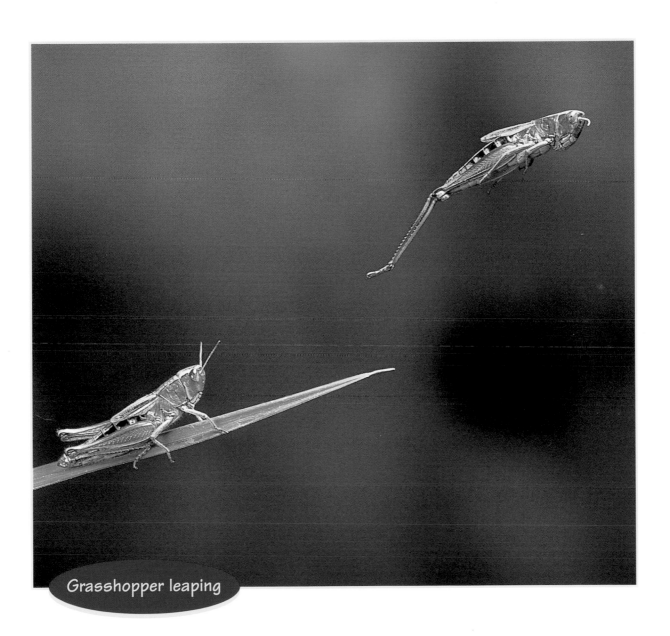

Grasshopper leaping

15

How Does a Grasshopper Breathe?

A grasshopper needs to breathe air—just as a person does. But grasshoppers don't have lungs. Instead, they have tiny holes, called spiracles, in their thoraxes and abdomens.

A grasshopper has 10 pairs of spiracles. Air goes into the insect's body through the front holes. Air leaves the body through the back holes. Next time you see a grasshopper, look at it closely. You will see its abdomen move in and out as it breathes.

Grasshopper

What Do Grasshoppers Eat?

Short-horned grasshoppers feed on plants. Some eat only certain kinds of plants. Others eat any plant they can find. Many grasshoppers eat clover, corn, cotton, soybeans, and other farm crops. Hungry grasshoppers sometimes eat a whole field of corn stalks—right down to the ground.

Most long-horned grasshoppers eat plants, too. However, some eat the remains of dead animals. A few even eat other insects.

Grasshoppers are very big eaters. A large group, or swarm, of grasshoppers can eat up entire fields of grain. Their huge appetites cause farmers a lot of trouble.

Short-horned
grasshopper

How Does a Grasshopper Make Music?

You know that a grasshopper has very powerful hind legs. These legs are good for leaping. But short-horned grasshoppers also use their legs to make music!

Short-horned grasshoppers sing by rubbing a hind leg against a front wing. It's a bit like playing a violin. The grasshopper's hind leg acts as the bow.

Many long-horned grasshoppers can sing, too. But they use their two front wings instead of their legs. One wing has a "file." The other wing has a "scraper." The grasshopper rubs these two parts together to make a song.

Male grasshoppers usually do all the singing. The females rarely make sounds. Males have several reasons for singing. They sing mostly to attract females. Males also make sounds to warn other kinds of insects to stay away. Some grasshoppers even make alarm calls when danger is near.

Short-horned
grasshopper singing

How Does a Grasshopper Lay Her Eggs?

Soon after grasshoppers mate, the female is ready to lay her eggs. She usually lays her eggs in the ground. A special body part called an ovipositor (OH vuh PAHZ uh tuhr) helps the female do this. The ovipositor is a tube from which the eggs pass out of the female's body. Before she lays her eggs, the female drills a hole in the soil. She uses her ovipositor to do this. Then she lays her eggs inside the hole. Each egg looks like a tiny grain of rice. The female may lay over a hundred eggs at one time.

After she lays the eggs, the female covers them with thick, sticky foam. The foam hardens and keeps the eggs from getting wet. The eggs and foam together are called a pod.

Female grasshopper
laying eggs

How Does a Baby Grasshopper Hatch?

Many grasshoppers lay their eggs in the fall. By the next spring, the eggs are ready to hatch. When a baby grasshopper hatches, it wiggles slowly out of its egg. Then it pushes through the egg pod and makes its way up out of the hole.

A baby grasshopper is called a nymph *(NIHMF)*. Nymphs look like little adult grasshoppers except for one thing—they don't have fully grown wings.

Nymphs may be tiny, but they have huge appetites. In fact, nymphs eat even more than adult grasshoppers do.

Nymph in pod

Why Does a Nymph Shed Its Skin?

Like its parents, a nymph has a hard exoskeleton. This exoskeleton cannot grow or stretch. So, as the nymph grows, it must shed its exoskeleton. This is called molting.

When a nymph is ready to molt, it climbs onto a leaf or a branch. It may even hang upside down. Slowly, the nymph slides out of its old exoskeleton. Underneath, the nymph has a new, soft exoskeleton. The nymph puffs up with air. This makes its body bigger while the new exoskeleton hardens. Now the nymph has room to grow until the next molt!

Most grasshoppers shed their skins 6 to 10 times. As they molt, most nymphs grow wings. The wings begin as little pads. They grow with each molt. The wings are finally formed by the time of the last molt.

Nymph molting

What Preys on Grasshoppers?

Spiders prey on grasshoppers. So do insects such as ants and mantids. Birds, monkeys, and snakes also make meals out of grasshoppers. And so do chameleons—like the one pictured here. That's a lot of enemies to look out for!

A grasshopper's eggs aren't safe either. Many insects enjoy eating grasshopper eggs. Young beetles will often move into an egg pod and stay there until they've eaten all the eggs. Some adult insects lay their own eggs inside a grasshopper's pod. When the babies of these insects are born, they feed on the grasshopper eggs.

Grasshopper as prey

29

How Do Grasshoppers Protect Themselves?

Grasshoppers have several ways to protect themselves. One way is by leaping. With their leaps, they can often jump away from their enemies. The grasshoppers simply leap up and fly away.

A grasshopper's coloring may also help to protect it. Some grasshoppers blend right in with their surroundings. For example, grasshoppers that live near green plants are often green.

The grasshopper you see here has a different approach. Instead of blending in, it really stands out. Often, brightly colored grasshoppers are poisonous. This grasshopper's bright colors warn enemies to stay away.

It may seem rude, but grasshoppers also spit to protect themselves. When a grasshopper is handled, it spits out a brown liquid. This foul stuff helps keep enemies away. A grasshopper may also use its strong jaws to bite an enemy.

Australian grasshopper

What Happens When Grasshoppers Swarm?

Grasshoppers usually live alone. But every so often, grasshoppers swarm, or form a large group.

Scientists aren't sure why grasshoppers swarm. They often swarm after many females have laid their eggs very close together. When the eggs hatch, there are nymphs leaping all over the place! For some reason, these nymphs often stay together. They begin to move about as one. Soon they become adults and form a flying swarm!

Sometimes swarms of short-horned grasshoppers migrate, or travel long distances. Short-horned grasshoppers that migrate are known as migratory locusts. These locusts may travel 25 to 50 miles (40 to 80 kilometers) a day. They may fly hundreds of miles before they are finished.

Locust nymphs

How Big Can a Locust Swarm Get?

Imagine billions and billions of insects flying overhead. That's how big a swarm of migratory locusts can be! The swarm can become so thick that it fills the sky and blocks out sunlight. The swarm can extend for thousands of miles.

Eventually the locusts in a swarm do land. Then they eat just about everything in sight. They mow through entire fields of crops.

In the past, swarms of locusts have formed in almost every part of the world. There have been large swarms in Africa, Australia, Europe, and the western United States. As you can imagine, passing through a swarm by car or plane can be dangerous!

Swarm of locusts

Who Calls Out Its Name?

"Katy did. Katy did." Many people think that's what a katydid mating call sounds like. Male katydids begin their songs as the sun sets. They often sing all night long!

A katydid is a type of long-horned grasshopper. Its feelers are very long—longer than its entire body. Many katydids are shaped like leaves. The veins on their wings even look like the veins of leaves.

Many katydids have sharp spines on their front legs. They use these spines to capture and kill prey. All katydids prey on other katydids and crickets—as well as other insects.

Katydid

Who Is That Brightly Colored 'Hopper?

It's a "monkey 'hopper," of course! The monkey grasshopper, which lives in tropical rain forests, is famous for its beautiful colors. Notice how this monkey 'hopper's head seems to shine. And look at all the different colors of its abdomen!

There are over 1,000 different kinds of monkey grasshoppers. But not all monkey 'hoppers are as striking as the one you see here. Some are mostly green, and these blend in with the colors of their rain forest homes.

Monkey grasshoppers have very short antennae and very long hind legs. Their hind legs are so long that when a monkey 'hopper sits on a leaf, its legs often splay, or spread out, to the sides.

Monkey 'hopper

Which Grasshopper Is a Thief?

Some farmers consider the Mormon cricket to be a thief. That's because this cricket steals feed from grazing lands in the western United States.

The Mormon cricket is not really a cricket. It's actually a long-horned grasshopper. But it does look like a field cricket. Both insects can be large and black. Both have long feelers. So how can you tell them apart? A Mormon cricket's wings are much smaller than a field cricket's wings. Because their wings are so small, Mormon crickets can't fly.

Mormon crickets seem to prefer the flower and seed parts of a plant. These are the same parts that cattle, sheep, and horses graze on. After Mormon crickets sweep through an area, little is left for farm animals to eat.

40

Mormon crickets

Just What Are Crickets?

Crickets are leaping insects that are closely related to long-horned grasshoppers. A male cricket sings, just as a male long-horned grasshopper does. When a cricket's front wings scrape together, they make a chirping sound. In fact, each species of cricket has a different song.

There are many different types of crickets, including mole crickets and leaf-rolling crickets. But the field cricket is one of the most familiar. It, along with the snowy tree cricket, belongs to the family of "true" crickets. Field crickets usually have front wing covers that lie flat on their backs. The covers fold down their sides like a tablecloth.

Field cricket

Do Crickets Make Good Pets?

For hundreds of years, people in parts of Asia have kept crickets as pets. Crickets are said to bring cheer and good luck to a home. They also provide lovely music.

The Chinese used to keep their pet crickets in small cages made of bamboo or wood. A cricket cage often contained tiny dishes for the insect's food and water. Sometimes an owner would even give the cricket a little clay bed to sleep on. The owners might tickle the cricket with a rabbit's whiskers to make it sing.

At one time, people in China walked around town with their pet crickets. Cricket owners often placed their pets in tiny containers, which they put in their pockets. People walking down a street in China could hear the cheery sound of crickets chirping.

Pet cricket

Which Crickets Sing from the Treetops?

On a summer night, you may hear the sound of "treet-treet-treet" coming from the trees. This is the high-pitched song of male tree crickets. These true crickets live high up in trees. Tree crickets often sing together—just like a choir.

Common field crickets are black. But tree crickets are white or pale green. Their thin, see-through wings make them look frail. But their songs really soar!

Tree crickets use their strong hind legs to hop from tree branch to tree branch. They feed mostly on very tiny insects called aphids *(AY fihdz)*. Aphids kill plants by sucking out their juices.

Tree cricket

Which Cricket Loves Ants?

It's the ant-loving cricket, of course! This wingless cricket is only 3/4 to 1 1/4 inches (19 to 32 millimeters) long.

The ant-loving cricket lives in the dry parts of the western United States. It spends most of its time in and around ant nests. As many as 50 of these crickets can be found in a single nest at one time. What are they doing there? These crickets are trying to steal a meal from their hosts!

To get food, the cricket approaches an ant. Then the cricket makes a series of motions. Somehow the motions persuade the ant to spit up a drop of food.

The ants do not like the crickets as much as the crickets like the ants. The ants try to drive their unwanted guests out—every chance they get.

Ant-loving cricket

Who Is Hiding in That Leaf?

Insects lead very dangerous lives. The world is just full of predators! Insects have to be very clever just to stay alive. They use camouflage *(KAM uh flahzh),* warning calls, stings, bites, foul odors, and other ways to protect themselves.

Insects known as leaf rollers protect themselves another way. They hide in little shelters that they make from leaves.

The leaf-rolling cricket shown here is a nocturnal insect. It feeds at night and rests or hides during the day. During the night, this cricket hunts aphids. But during the day, the leaf-rolling cricket hides out in a homemade shelter. This cricket makes its shelter by rolling up a leaf. Then it ties the leaf with a silklike thread from its mouth.

Leaf-rolling cricket

Which Crickets Are Spelunkers?

Have you ever explored a cave? If you have, you're a spelunker *(spih LUHNG kuhr)*—a person who explores caves. And if you've ever explored a Texas cave, you may have seen—but not heard—the secret cave cricket.

Cave crickets are silent and wingless. Scientists do not classify them as "true" crickets. Cave crickets have very long antennae, and their long back legs make them excellent leapers.

The secret cave cricket that lives in Texas is little—no longer than 1 inch (2.5 centimeters). This cricket likes company. It can live in groups of up to 5,000 members! Cave crickets are not very fussy about their food. When night comes, these crickets leave the caves and eat anything they find!

52

Secret cave cricket

Is That a Camel in the Basement?

The spotted camel cricket has a hump. And it has the word *camel* in its name. But that's about all this insect has in common with a camel. Camels live on plains and in deserts. But spotted camel crickets prefer cool, damp caves—or even basements.

Did you ever see a dark brown cricket in a basement? If so, it may have been a spotted camel cricket. This insect commonly invades homes in the central and eastern United States and Canada.

Like the secret cave cricket, the spotted camel cricket has no wings. It is not a "true" cricket. But it is an excellent leaper, and it has very long antennae. If an enemy comes along, the antennae alert the cricket to the danger.

Spotted camel cricket

Can a Cricket Dig a Burrow?

If it's a mole cricket, it certainly can! This insect is like a well-designed digging machine. It has short, shovellike front legs. It also has a pointy head and a coat of fine hair. The hair keeps soil from sticking to its body as it digs.

Mole crickets are usually brown or black. They are about 1 to 2 inches (2.5 to 5.0 centimeters) long. The female lays her eggs in tunnels near the roots of plants. When the eggs hatch, the nymphs join the adults in eating the roots. The West Indian mole cricket—or changa as it is called in Puerto Rico—eats the roots of sugar cane. This hungry insect can cause a lot of damage to crops.

Although mole crickets live underground, they have wings and can fly. They often come to the surface on warm nights or when the soil is wet.

West Indian
mole cricket

What Are Wetas?

Wetas are rare insects that live in New Zealand. Wetas have been around over 100 million years! That means they were around at the time of the dinosaurs. Scientists think that wetas today look much the same as they did back then.

Wetas are large insects. They can be longer than 3 inches (7.5 centimeters). Their large size comes in handy, too. Many of the islands where wetas live do not have small mammals. So wetas actually fill the roles of mammals such as mice, shrews, and rats.

Wetas are mostly meat-eaters. They eat other insects, such as beetles. They eat earthworms, too. But, like mice and rats, wetas will eat just about anything.

Cave weta

Are These Animals in Danger?

For the most part, orthoptera are not in danger. They can be found almost all over the world. In fact, orthoptera are doing so well that people often try to get rid of them. Farmers use sprays and pesticides to try to control their numbers.

But some of the grasshopper's relatives are in danger. In New Zealand, rats have accidentally been released. The rats have nearly wiped out some kinds of wetas. Now, scientists are trying to get rid of the rats and save the wetas.

The habitats of other orthoptera are in danger, too. Many rain forests around the world are being cut down. When rain forests are cut down, many of these insects lose their homes.

But, in the end, there are billions of grasshoppers and their relatives. And they have been around for millions of years. It is safe to say they will be leaping around for many more!

Grasshopper

Fun Facts

→ Long-horned grasshoppers and crickets have an ear on each of their two front legs.

→ In just one day, a swarm of locusts can eat as much as all the citizens of New York City, London, Los Angeles, and Paris combined eat in a day.

→ A cricket can clean itself while it sings.

→ Some kinds of grasshoppers smell really bad—and that's good. Their rotten odors keep their enemies away.

→ Count the number of times a snowy tree cricket chirps in 15 seconds. Then add 40 to this number. That will tell you what the temperature is outside.

Glossary

abdomen The third part of an insect's body.

antennae The feelers on an insect's head.

cold-blooded Having a body temperature that changes with the environment.

compound eye An eye made up of many separate lenses.

exoskeleton A tough, outer body covering.

migrate To move from one region to another, especially at a particular time of year.

molt To lose fur, skin, or another body covering before getting a new one.

nocturnal Active at night.

nymph An insect that is in the development stage between egg and adult.

orthoptera An order of insects that includes grasshoppers, katydids, and crickets.

orthopteron An insect that belongs to the order orthoptera.

ovipositor The tube from which the eggs pass out of a grasshopper's body.

pod A grasshopper's eggs and foam together.

swarm A large group of insects flying or moving together.

spelunker A person who explores caves.

spiracles Breathing holes on a grasshopper's abdomen and thorax.

thorax The second part of an insect's body, between the head and abdomen.

63

Index

(**Boldface** indicates a photo or illustration.)

For more information about Grasshoppers and Their Relatives, try these resources:

Crickets and Grasshoppers, by Ann O. Squire,
  Children's Press, 2003

Grasshoppers, by Ann Heinrichs, Compass Point
  Books, 2002

Life of a Grasshopper, by Clare Hibbert, Raintree, 2004

http://buzz.ifas.ufl.edu

http://forums.insecthobbyist.com/forum.php?
catid=13

http://www.insects.org/entophiles/orthoptera/

Orthoptera Classification

Scientists classify animals by placing them into groups. The animal kingdom is a group that contains all the world's animals. Phylum, class, order, and family are smaller groups. Each phylum contains many classes. A class contains orders, and a family contains individual species. Each species also has its own scientific name. Here is how the animals in this book fit in to this system.

Insects and their relatives (Phylum Arthropoda)

Insects (Class Insecta)

Grasshoppers and their relatives (Order Orthoptera)

Ant-loving crickets (Family Myrmecophilidae)

Camel and cave crickets (Family Rhaphidophoridae)

Secret cave cricket . . . . *Ceuthophilus secretus*

Spotted camel cricket . . . . *Ceuthophilus maculatus*

Crickets (Family Gryllidae)

Field cricket . . . . *Gryllus pennsylvanicus*

Snowy tree cricket . . . . *Oecanthus fultoni*

Grasshoppers and locusts (Family Acrididae)

Katydids and other long-horned grasshoppers (Family Tettigoniidae)

Mormon cricket . . . . *Anabrus simplex*

Leaf-rolling crickets (Family Gryllacrididae)

Leaf-rolling cricket . . . . *Camptonotus carolinensis*

Mole crickets . . . . *Gryllotalpidae*

Monkey grasshoppers (Family Eumastiacidae)